IMAGES
of America

HANOVER TOWNSHIP

WHIPPANY AND CEDAR KNOLLS

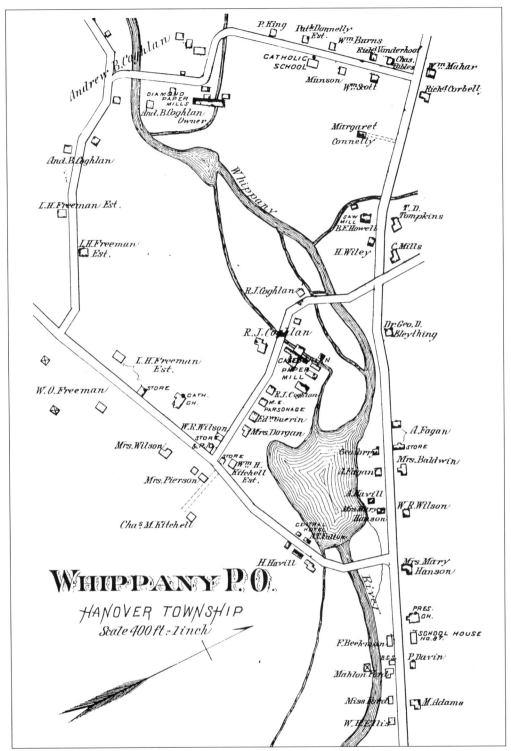

This map of the Village of Whippany from *Robinson's Atlas of Morris County, New Jersey* was published in 1887.

2

IMAGES
of America

HANOVER TOWNSHIP
WHIPPANY AND CEDAR KNOLLS

Steven P. Hepler and Robert F. Krygoski

ARCADIA

First published 1998
Copyright © Steven P. Hepler and Robert F. Krygoski, 1998

ISBN 0-7524-0976-X

Published by Arcadia Publishing,
an imprint of the Chalford Publishing Corporation,
One Washington Center, Dover, New Hampshire 03820.
Printed in Great Britain

Library of Congress Cataloging-in-Publication Data applied for

History is the ship carrying living memories to the future.

—Stephen Spender

Contents

Introduction

The first recorded evidence of explorers and settlers locating along the banks of the Whippany River in Hanover Township can be traced back to 1685. According to the New Jersey Historical Society's *Early History of Morris County, New Jersey* (1869), ". . . it is said to have been the earliest settlement within the limits of present-day Morris and Sussex Counties." Documents from 1710 indicate that these early settlers came from Newark, New Jersey (settled in 1666), and Long Island, New York. They found their way to what would become Hanover Township by way of present-day Livingston and Caldwell.

Of course, the Lenni-Lenape Indians were the first known individuals in this region. No one knows where they originally came from, but the Whippany River, named "Whippanong" (or "Many Willows") by the Lenni-Lenape, is what originally attracted them to the area. To them, the Whippanong meant life; to Hanover Township millwrights of the mid-18th to late 19th centuries, it meant industrial power. Gristmills, sawmills, cotton mills, and, ultimately, paper mills sprang up along the Whippany River. Eventually the paper mills would rise as the dominant industry and put the village of Whippany on the map. Indeed, for many years, a large sign in the center of town proudly stated "Whippany Makes Paper; Paper Makes Whippany."

Geographically, Hanover was the largest township in the state of New Jersey and encompassed all of the territory that is now part of Morris, Sussex, and Warren Counties. As new municipalities formed from 1740 to 1928, Hanover shrank little by little until its vast size was reduced to its current 10.8 square miles. In 1810 the township's population was recorded at 3,843. In 1900 it totaled 5,366; in 1930, 2,516; in 1960, 9,329; and today there are approximately 15,000 persons residing in Hanover Township.

This book will in no way attempt to cover the entire history of Hanover Township. That was notably done in the highly regarded *Along the Whippanong* by Elizabeth R. Myrose and Claire B. Kitchell in 1966. That book, which allowed us to check many of our facts, unfortunately has long been out of print. It is hoped that the photographic images contained within these pages will celebrate the rich history of the region with a touch of nostalgia for what has gone before. For longtime residents, we hope to rekindle fond memories of a quieter time "along the Whippanong." For newer residents and visitors, this presentation will introduce you to a Hanover not to be forgotten, a Hanover to be cherished and remembered.

As we finished work on this book, it became apparent that there would be a large number of unused photographs. A second volume is planned in which we anticipate including much of what could not make it into this initial work. Additionally, we would welcome hearing from people who have photographs and information that they would be willing to share for Volume II of *Hanover Township*. Interested persons may contact us at the following address: Bob Krygoski, PO Box 304, Whippany, NJ 07981.

Steven P. Hepler
Robert F. Krygoski
March 12, 1998

Acknowledgments

We would like to extend our thanks and appreciation to the many fine individuals and organizations who kindly gave us assistance or lent the material that makes up this book.

Tony Russomanno resided in Whippany for over 60 years. In the mid-1920s he started to work for Jensen's Gasoline part time, and by the mid-1940s he had purchased the building (once located on Route 10 West and Whippany Road) and began the Whippany Filling Station. Until his retirement in the early 1970s, Tony witnessed many changes in town and saw many people come and go.

Tony captured many pieces of history with his camera. He would be called upon by the local authorities to take photographs at police investigations and then rush back to his darkroom that was set up at the filling station to develop the pictures. When Tony was cleaning out the station in preparation for retirement, Steve Bolcar, officer of the Hanover Township Police Department, stopped by. Steve saw Tony going toward the garbage with his over 2,000 old negatives, and thankfully Steve had the foresight to save and preserve these for 26 years. When we started this project we were very fortunate that Steve lent the negatives to us.

We spoke with Tony during the making of this book. He and his daughter, Ruth Kollmar, who lives in Florida, were very helpful in supplying facts and additional photographs.

Richard and Scott Bradley, owners of the Bradley-Braviak Funeral Home, were very generous in donating office space for the organization of the book at their business. The Bradleys are also interested in preserving the town's history. Richard's collection of old maps of Hanover can be seen hanging on the walls of the funeral home.

Special thanks goes to Linda Byrne, Don Kiddoo, and John Paustian of the Hanover Township Landmark Committee for giving us complete access to the committee's collection of archival photographs, which were essential to this project.

During the process of collecting photographs and information for our book we had the pleasure of meeting with many people, among them Donald and Claire Kitchell. Claire, who was one of our local historians, also co-wrote *Along the Whippanong* in 1966 with the late Elizabeth R. Myrose. Claire identified unknown photographs and supplied us with important facts and was very anxious to see the finished product. Unfortunately, she passed away during the final days of this project and we were very saddened. Our thoughts go out to Don and to her children and grandchildren, most of whom reside in Whippany.

Tricia L. Schoeneck of the Morristown Municipal Airport enthusiastically provided us with a great selection of publicity photographs and old newspaper clippings. Carol Gray at The Seeing Eye in Morristown, New Jersey, generously supplied photographs taken during the period when the famous guide-dog school was headquartered in Whippany. Patrice Edwards at Lucent Archives in Murray Hill, New Jersey, forwarded a unique selection of photographs of Bell Telephone Laboratories' Whippany facility during the 1950s. Marie Heagney at the Morris County Library allowed us access to postcards from the library's New Jersey Collection.

For the chapter on the Morristown & Erie Railroad, we were fortunate to obtain material from not only the present-day Morristown & Erie Railway and the Whippany Railway Museum, but also from two individuals who photographed the railroad many times in the 1930s and '40s. Thanks to both Homer R. Hill of Bernardsville, New Jersey, and Donald Van Court of Madison, New Jersey, for the use of their photographs. Bob Pennisi of Long Valley, New Jersey, also provided photographs from his Railroad Avenue Enterprises Collection. [For those residents who would like to know more about their "hometown" railroad, which has over a century of friendly service to its credit, a separate work-in-progress by Steve Hepler, entitled *Rails through the Hanover Hills*, will be released by Arcadia early in 1999; it will take the reader on a photographic journey across the 11-mile line between Morristown, Whippany, and Essex Fells.]

We could not believe our luck when John Durkota proudly invited us to view the collection of photographs he took while employed at the McEwan Brothers' Eden Mill in the 1930s and 1940s. Many people have been searching for paper mill scenes since the mills closed in 1980; within this book are a few of those treasured images.

Additionally, we would like to extend our sincere thanks to the many township residents, friends, and family who supplied us with photographs and memories: Joe and Fran Braviak, Susan J. Braviak, Fred Brunner, Gene and Betty Clemens, Jim Davidson, Sonny and Mutz DeLukey, Bob Kasiski, Richard Kitchell, Frank and Ronnie Krygoski, Haide Krygoski, Joe Mihalko, Vin Minner, Frank Reda, Joe Salinari, John Sharry, Clifford Welsh, and Val Yesenko.

Polhemus Hall and Store, located at Route 10 East and Troy Hills Road, still stands today slightly altered from its original state. This view was captured in the 1890s. In 1898, the Polhemus Store was noted as having the first telephone exchange in Whippany. The Polhemus daughters served as the first telephone operators. (Photograph courtesy of Donald Kitchell.)

One
Gone but Not Forgotten

At the intersection of Route 10 and Whippany Road a traveler would come upon this scene of Tony Russomanno's Whippany Filling Station and Mauritius Jensen's home. Tony was the unofficial township photographer and he is responsible for many of the photographs that appear in this book. In addition to selling gasoline and related products here, Tony set up a darkroom within this classic American gas station. (Photograph courtesy of Tony Russomanno.)

The Whippany Filling Station was originally owned by the Jensens, who lived next door. The authors have been told that Jensen had 10 pumps at this small station, all offering diverse brands of petrol. After Tony Russomanno took over, the station became a Texaco outlet. A motorist could also obtain newspapers, magazines, soft drinks, and ice cream at the "periodicals" store on the right side of the station. (Photograph courtesy of Tony Russomanno.)

An early car wash system was set up within the service bays of the Whippany Filling Station during the later years of Tony Russomanno's ownership. We are confident that most vehicles were washed and rinsed efficiently, but wonder about the efficacy of the drying process. Note the two fans hanging above this Dodge station wagon. (Photograph courtesy of Tony Russomanno.)

The Moore Brick Manufacturing Co. was started in Whippany in 1899 and bricks made of stiff mud were produced here. The plant was not successful, however, and in 1903 it was reorganized as the Hanover Brick Co. under McEwan control. The facility closed in 1931, after another attempt at reorganization in 1921. Where 60,000 bricks were once produced daily, today stands the township swimming pool. (Photograph courtesy of Hanover Township Landmark Committee.)

Betty's Restaurant, which served Italian food, was once located on Route 10 East near Ridgedale Avenue. Howard Johnson's presently occupies the site. Note the c. 1950 billboard with the Nash automobile advertisement to the left of the structure. (Photograph courtesy of Tony Russomanno.)

Mauritius Jensen's home was photographed on February 8, 1962, and was located at the intersection of Route 10 and Whippany Road adjacent to the Whippany Filling Station. This elegant Victorian home was razed on February 10, 1964, to make way for the present-day Whippany Road jughandle that now encircles the Whippany Filling Station's successor, Exxon Gasoline. (Photograph courtesy of Tony Russomanno.)

Above is a February 2, 1962, scene from Mauritius Jensen's backyard. Alongside the back of the barn are the tracks of the Morristown & Erie (M & E) Railroad. Today all of the property seen here is owned by the M & E and the area to the right side of the photograph where the barn was once located has been turned into a parking lot. (Photograph courtesy of Tony Russomanno.)

This 1910 postcard view depicts Robert B. McEwan Jr.'s 50-acre Whippany Road estate. In 1931, this impressive Victorian became the headquarters of The Seeing Eye, where dogs were trained to guide blind persons. In 1965, The Seeing Eye relocated to Morristown and the entire estate was demolished when the property was acquired by Bell Labs. (Photograph courtesy of the collection of Vin Minner.)

The idyllic surroundings of the front lawn of the Whippany depot of the M & E were photographed on February 8, 1962, from Mauritius Jensen's backyard. Today, most of the park-like setting has been replaced by the Whippany Road jughandle and a parking lot. (Photograph courtesy of Tony Russomanno.)

This sawmill—once owned by the Fairchild family in the 1800s—was located on the east side of North Jefferson Road across from the Hanover Township Community Center. (Photograph courtesy of Hanover Township Landmark Committee.)

Old Distillery and Mill, Whippany, N. J.

1432

This gristmill, one of two 19th-century mills in Hanover Township, was once owned by the Shipmans. It was located on Route 10 West across from the present-day Pine Plaza shopping center. Later, one of the Shipmans became the second postmaster of Whippany. (Photograph courtesy of Hanover Township Landmark Committee.)

This two-lane dirt road that once passed through Hanover Township would now be identified as Route 10 in Whippany. The stately home of W.F. Ager once stood across from the 19th-century gristmill near the present site of Whippany Sand and Gravel. (Photograph courtesy of the New Jersey Collection of the Morris County Library.)

This photograph taken in the very early years of Whippany looks west on what would be Route 10 from Ridgedale Avenue in East Hanover. Today this area of highway houses businesses such as Gold's Gym and Anchor Golfland. (Photograph courtesy of Hanover Township Landmark Committee.)

In its day, Whippany Coal, Feed and Supply provided heating fuels to local residents. This c. 1940s photograph shows the office/scale house once located on Parsippany Road across from the Whippany Post Office. The building on the left side in the rear remains today, slightly altered and used for storage. (Photograph courtesy of Hanover Township Landmark Committee.)

Nelson's Corner, housed on the lower level of the two-story structure that once stood on the corner of Parsippany and Whippany Roads, was a popular lunch spot c. 1950s. A private residence was maintained above. Today, Corestates Bank is located on this site. (Photograph courtesy of Tony Russomanno.)

This *c.* 1800s photograph shows the Fagan house on Route 10 West, just west of Whippany Road and just east of the railroad crossing. Mr. William Fagan, the first funeral director in the township, started his business about 1910 and closed in the late 50s. Very few funerals were actually held in this home. Prior to 1960, it was not uncommon to have the funeral service in the deceased's home. (Photograph courtesy of Donald Kitchell.)

The Frazier house, one of many large homes along Whippany Road, is seen here in the 1950s. It was demolished to provide room for the present Emmanual Lutheran Church on the corner of Whippany Road and Park Avenue. (Photograph courtesy of Tony Russomanno.)

Built in the late 1700s, this building assumed a variety of names: Tappans Tavern, Whippany Hotel, Martin House, and Parsons Still. In the late 1960s a fire destroyed most of the unoccupied structure, which was later demolished. On the site today at Route 10 and Troy Hills Road stands a Lone Star Steak House. (Photograph courtesy of Tony Russomanno.)

The Our Lady of Mercy Church Hall, a Quonset-type building located in the left rear of the chapel parking lot, opened on April 18, 1949. Many church social functions would be held here over the years. The building was also used for school plays and gym class. (Photograph courtesy of Tony Russomanno.)

The first municipal building in Hanover Township is pictured here on the left. The Whipponong Hall, as it was called, housed all the town records and a small library of books. The small building on the right was Whippany's third post office location. In 1909 the town hall was razed by a fire that destroyed all records. On this site today stands Whippany's post office. (Photograph courtesy of Hanover Township Landmark Committee.)

This large home once located across from Corporate Communications Group on Parsippany Road was originally the home of Daniel Coghlan in 1848. Daniel, who was an industrial leader in the community associated with the paper mills, also let Roman Catholics use his home for mass until their own chapel was built on Whippany Road. That chapel still stands today. (Photograph courtesy of Hanover Township Landmark Committee.)

Richard W. McEwan Sr. lived in this home, which stood at the entrance to Hanover Mill at the intersection of Route 10 and Whippany Road. Richard was president of the Morristown & Erie Railroad. He passed away on April 15, 1936, and his wife, the former Hanna Brown, died in 1938. This photograph was taken at her funeral. (Photograph courtesy of Hanover Township Landmark Committee.)

This c. 1800s home that once stood on the corner of Whippany and Parsippany Roads at the present site of the Gulf Gas Station was the home and office of Dr. McCormick. Note the large wraparound porch with the car porte cochere on the right side. (Photograph courtesy of Donald Kitchell.)

Among the homes on Whippany Road there were also several eating establishments. Seen here *c.* 1940s is Archies, a popular roadside restaurant where one could dine very casually. Later this building was remodeled for the Acres Restaurant. The site today is home to the Whippany Park High School tennis courts. (Photograph courtesy of the collection of R.F. Krygoski.)

When Archies closed another popular eatery opened, serving hot dogs, hamburgers, and pizza on the corner of Whippany Road and Druetzler Court. In the mid-60s a fire destroyed most of the structure and it could not be rebuilt. (Photograph courtesy of the collection of R.F. Krygoski.)

This postcard view illustrates the elegant Acres Restaurant, once situated on the former site of Archies on Whippany Road. Customers would travel from afar for the Acres' fine cuisine. Over the years the building underwent many renovations. The Acres was razed by fire in the early 1960s. (Photograph courtesy of the collection of R.F. Krygoski.)

THE FARMSTEAD, WHIPPANY, N.J.

This 1881 home of George Freeman later became the Farmstead restaurant, located on the west side of Whippany Road between the Our Lady of Mercy Church and Chapel. This structure also served as the convent for many years until it was demolished to make way for the Oak Ridge Condominiums. (Photograph courtesy of the collection of Steven Hepler.)

Two
All Around the Town

Residents are seen enjoying an outing at an unknown spot in Hanover Township. Driving Walter Adamson's 1904 Cadillac was his sister Sara. Walter purchased this car from Jesse McEwan for $600 in 1905. At that time his automobile was one of three vehicles in town. (Photograph courtesy of the collection of R.F. Krygoski.)

On a warm sunny day, local children and a gentleman wait for the parade to pass by their location at Route 10 across from the Whippany firehouse. Pictured standing from left to right are Bob Kasiski, Sonny De Lukey, and Tony Kasiski; in the wagon are George De Lukey, Jack Kasiski, and Ruth Russomanno. (Photograph courtesy of Tony Russomanno.)

Everyone loves a parade! Here, a group of Whippany schoolchildren assembles with drums, hats, and ribbons to celebrate some long-forgotten holiday, perhaps Memorial Day. The little boy second from left is wearing a Gingerbread Castle T-shirt. An original today would most likely command a high price in the collectibles marketplace. (Photograph courtesy of Tony Russomanno.)

Members of the Welsh family and their friends posed for this photograph before the wedding ceremony of Eugene Clemens and Betty Welsh. On the front lawn at 15 Parsippany Road are, from left to right, Marion Mills, Mrs. Liepert, Betty Welsh, Emma (Carrol) Welsh, and Estelle Peele. On April 26, 1941, Betty and Eugene married; they currently reside at 17 Parsippany Road. (Photograph courtesy of Eugene Clemens.)

A Mardi Gras celebration was held at Saint John's Ukrainian Hall. What makes this photograph all the more interesting are not so much the costumed revelers (although there are some rather unusual characters here), but the business advertisements adorning the upper walls of the hall. Look for Tony Russomanno's Whippany Filling Station, the McEwan Brothers' Eden Mills, Glover Dairy Farms, Michael Konesny's Plumbing & Heating, and William Polhemus General Insurance. (Photograph courtesy of Tony Russomanno.)

The next five photographs depict the May 30, 1951 Whippany Memorial Day Parade as seen through the camera lens of Tony Russomanno. Here, marching east along the three-lane Route 10 past the Whippany Filling Station and Mauritius Jensen's home, are a flag-carrying troop of Girl Scouts. Vehicular traffic continues to flow westbound but the eastbound and passing lanes are temporarily reserved for paraders. (Photograph courtesy of Tony Russomanno.)

The Whippany Fire Company carries the colors high as its volunteer members march eastbound along Route 10. (Photograph courtesy of Tony Russomanno.)

The Cedar Knolls Fire Department takes its place in Whippany's May 30, 1951 Memorial Day Parade. The color guard leads the procession along Thomas Street (Parsippany Road) and its members in front are crossing the bridge over Stony Brook. Those in the middle are crossing the Morristown & Erie tracks and the Whippany River Bridge just beyond the railroad. (Photograph courtesy of Tony Russomanno.)

Our Lady of Mercy (OLM) cadets smartly carry the colors as they participate in the Whippany Memorial Day Parade. Following behind and just out focus is the OLM drum and bugle corps. (Photograph courtesy of Tony Russomanno.)

Members of the Whippany Fire Company travel in style in the May 30, 1951 Memorial Day Parade. Who among us today wouldn't love to own one of these classic American automobiles or one of the equally classic and historic fire engines following behind? Come to think of it, the bunting-bedecked bicycle that youngster is riding on to the left is probably a classic now too! (Photograph courtesy of Tony Russomanno.)

All good parades must come to an end. Standing at School Street and Route 10 are several members of the Coolack family who enjoyed the May 30, 1951 Memorial Day Parade in Whippany. At the rear left are Paul Coolack, Susie Coolack, and Anna (Coolack) Stevens with baby Suzanne. In the front row from left to right are Jane Coolack, Sherwood Stevens, Carol (Stevens) Treible, and John DeLukey. (Photograph courtesy of Tony Russomanno.)

In the mid- to late 1950s, if people needed a football, tennis racquet, or other piece of sport-related gear they would go downtown to Guinter's Army Navy Store. Located at Route 10 East at the intersection of Troy Hills Road, the site is occupied today by C.B.S. Beauty Supply. Pictured here are Ben Guinter (left), his son Bob (right), and Bob's children. (Photograph courtesy of Tony Russomanno.)

Inside the Tibus Chevrolet dealership in front of one of the latest automobiles are the mechanics and parts men. Standing from left to right are Jack ?, John Tibus (owner), Ted Bluin, and John Yavorski. Kneeling from left to right are John Maluk, John Bolcar, and Mr. Carmin. This dealership was located on Route 10 East across from Fritze and Sons. (Photograph courtesy of the collection of R.F. Krygoski.)

Remember the radio public service announcement that admonished listeners, "Don't cross the street in the middle of the block . . ."? Tony Russomanno's camera captured a Reynolds Avenue school crossing guard protecting several children and their mother against vehicular traffic long before that classic jingle made its New York radio debut in 1961. (Photograph courtesy of Tony Russomanno.)

Three Cub Scouts from Pack 42 showed the trophies they won at the Pinewood Derby. The scouts would spend nights and weekends building their own car by carving, sanding, and painting a block of wood. When the cars were complete, the track would be set up in the Presbyterian church. The cars were powered only by gravity. (Photograph courtesy of Tony Russomanno.)

In August 1957, the New Jersey gubernatorial race was beginning to heat up. In what was probably just one of many such campaign dinners, then-Governor Robert Meyner attended festivities in Hanover to "press the flesh" in the hopes of gaining additional voter support. Standing from left to right are Frank Glackin, Governor Meyner, and Joe Foley. The dark-haired woman seated behind the flowers is Mrs. Meyner. (Photograph courtesy of Tony Russomanno.)

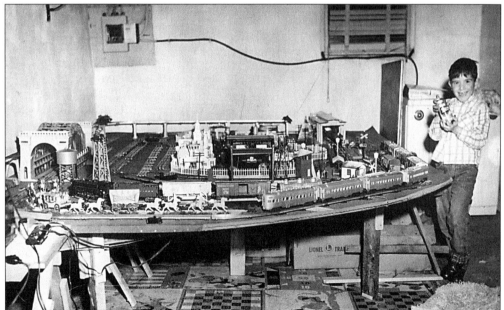

In Whippany and indeed in thousands of homes across America, *the* toys for boys (and their dads, uncles, and grandfathers) in the 1950s were Lionel Trains. Butchy Russomanno gets ready to spray some artificial snow on his basement layout in preparation for the upcoming Christmas holiday. (Photograph courtesy of Tony Russomanno.)

On the front lawn of the Morristown & Erie station stood several majestic pine trees. For many years one in particular would be decorated for the holidays. This 1956 night scene showing a festive mantle of snow set the mood for many township residents who eagerly awaited Santa's yearly arrival at the depot to hand out goodies to the children. (Photograph courtesy of Tony Russomanno.)

The Whippany firehouse shines brightly in the night during the 1956 Christmas season. Volunteer members Dick Glackin and Frank Krygoski annually decorated the building in this manner. Glackin was a well-known local sign painter and it was his artistic abilities that enabled this seasonal theme to be created and enjoyed by all. (Photograph courtesy of Tony Russomanno.)

A few days prior to Santa's annual arrival at the Whippany depot, several people would gather at the station and form an assembly line to quickly stuff hundreds of old-style netted Christmas stockings with candies and fruits donated by local merchants. This line-up of volunteers is from the 1956 season. Today this tradition is carried on by the local VFW. (Photograph courtesy of Tony Russomanno.)

A heavy snowfall did little to dampen the spirits of the crowd gathered at the Whippany station as they awaited Santa's arrival in 1956. The Christmas stockings have been filled, the parents have arrived with their children, and the tree is lit on the great lawn. Santa's grand entrance is at hand and the anticipation is building. (Photograph courtesy of Tony Russomanno.)

This Christmas 1957 scene shows hundreds of residents lined up at the Morristown & Erie's Whippany station to wait for the arrival of Santa Claus. Note the small, rustic, stone arch bridges over the channel that fed from the natural pond across the lawn, under Route 10 and on out to the Whippany River. The white-washed rocks outline the passageway to the depot. (Photograph courtesy of Tony Russomanno.)

Another late 1950s Christmas panorama at Whippany station captures the sun setting low over Konesny's Hardware Store on the right and the huge crowd of people encircling the frozen duck pond, upon which several people can be seen skating. The arrival of Santa Claus is imminent . . . the holidays are about to begin in Hanover. (Photograph courtesy of Tony Russomanno.)

The long expected appearance of Santa Claus at Whippany was achieved this time not by sleigh and reindeer, but by means of a pony-drawn carriage. Santa will make his way to the porte cochere of the station, where one by one he will greet the children and hand out the treat-filled stockings. We are sure many residents still smile at the thought of these magical childhood memories down at the depot. (Photograph courtesy of Tony Russomanno.)

This little girl has her stocking in hand, filled with apples, oranges, and candies. Santa speaks with each child and sends him or her along with a kind word. Today, The Whippany Railway Museum operates a train ride with Santa Claus on board. Passengers ride the rails of the M & E as Santa walks through the coaches with Christmas greetings and treats for everyone. (Photograph courtesy of Tony Russomanno.)

Mr. and Mrs. Mauritius Jensen were photographed by Tony Russomanno in the backyard of their home on Route 10 and Whippany Road in 1962. Mr. Jensen had been the auditor of the Morristown & Erie until his retirement on October 1, 1945. He continued to act as a vice president of the railroad until his death in February 1966 at the age of 90. (Photograph courtesy of Tony Russomanno.)

Mrs. Nora MacDonald Sias (1887–1951), editor and publisher of the *Whippany Advance*, lived in Whippany for 30 years. She founded the *Whippany Advance*, the first edition appearing in 1931. The studio office of the newspaper was on Reynolds Avenue. Mrs. Sias is seen at her desk being assisted by her French Shepherd dog, Jack Smith, who helped in producing every issue until he died. (Photograph courtesy of Whippany Fire Company.)

Three
Neighborhood
Merchants

The Whippany Filling Station was the first gas station in Hanover Township until the early 1930s. It was started in 1917 by Mauritius Jensen Jr. In the 1920s Anthony "Tony" Russomanno started to work for Jensen, and in the mid-40s he purchased the station and operated it until 1972. At the Route 10 and Whippany Road site now stands an Exxon service station. (Photograph courtesy of Tony Russomanno.)

The Shell gasoline station on Route 10 East and Whippany Road made use of an English Cottage-style design. By offering up hearth and home with its distinctive chimney and gabled roof, it promised an atmosphere that was appealing to weary motorists. The station still functions as a Shell franchise today, but this home-like building is no more. (Photograph courtesy of Tony Russomanno.)

Wainwright's Esso Servicenter was clad in gleaming white porcelain enamel tile, a material perfectly suited for use in gas stations. Based on a 1940s Streamline Moderne design, the building's oversize glass service bay doors were a trademark of a new style of gas station architecture. This station was located on Route 10 West just before the Parsippany Road overpass. Today a Mobil franchise occupies the site. (Photograph courtesy of Tony Russomanno.)

The Calso gasoline station at the corner of Whippany and Parsippany Roads survives today as a Gulf station. The remarkable fact is that except for color, signage, and the brand of gas sold , the station has changed little. But, a 1990s facelift is on the horizon. Gas station enthusiasts, get your photographs now! (Photograph courtesy of Tony Russomanno.)

The Minnisink Oil Company was established in 1927 to distribute Sun Oil Products including fuel oil and gasoline. An integral part of this firm was Jack's Sunoco service station as seen in this early 1960s view. Today, although the Sunoco station has moved a few yards west of this site on Route 10, the main building endures as the office of Petro Heating Oil & Services. (Photograph courtesy of Hanover Township Landmark Committee.)

In 1940, Suburban Gas Company started its operation. With just six employees at first, the plant served a few homes in the township. Almost 60 years later the company still serves the community and numerous industrial plants. (Photograph courtesy of Hanover Township Landmark Committee.)

The Braviak Funeral Home has been considered a notable landmark in Whippany for over 40 years and still serves the community today as the Bradley-Braviak Funeral Home. Joseph P. Braviak opened his business on January 2, 1956, and over the years has done remodeling to enhance the structure. The business is on the first-floor level and the private residence is on the second floor. (Photograph courtesy of J.P. Braviak.)

On December 27, 1927, the First National Bank of Whippany was formed by 13 prominent local men. As the community grew, so did the bank, and in 1948 the building doubled in size. In May of 1961 a second branch was opened in Cedar Knolls on Ridgedale Avenue. Today the bank building remains at the intersection of Route 10 and Whippany Roads. (Photograph courtesy of Hanover Township Landmark Committee.)

One of the few small diners in Whippany, Johnny's Diner—seen here in the mid-50s—catered to the blue-collar workforce. The truck drivers from the local mills and others could often be found ordering "today's specials" for lunch. Presently Frank's Diner operates at the same spot. (Photograph courtesy of Tony Russomanno.)

This c. mid-1950s photograph shows a dry cleaner and tailor in front of the present-day site of Billy & Madeline's Red Room. Billy's father Phillip first opened Phil's Tavern in the rented space behind the cleaners in 1933. After purchasing the building in 1945 from the Lefkowitz family, Phil ran the business until his son Billy took over in 1959. It became Billy's Red Room until 1980. (Photograph courtesy of Tony Russomanno.)

Flynn's Tavern on Route 10 West opened for business on January 3, 1954. Flynn's business originally began across the highway in a smaller building. With offices on the second floor, Dr. William P. McCrea opened his dental practice in March of 1954 and served the community until 1959 before moving to Convent Station. Presently Fritze & Sons own the building. (Photograph courtesy of Tony Russomanno.)

In 1957 the last stop for the Whippany Post Office before it opened its new building in 1962 on Parsippany Road was 622 Route 10 West, presently the site of Finelli's Pizza. This building, originally constructed as a bank, later became an auto parts store and a video store. (Photograph courtesy of Tony Russomanno.)

Pictured sorting the mail above in this 1940s photograph are, from left to right, Jim Tighe, Ella M. Fables (postmaster), Gerard Bisson, Anna Fables, and Eleanor (Konesny) Zailo. The Whippany Post Office, which had numerous branches in town when this photograph was taken, shared a building with Konesny's Hardware on Route 10 East, presently The Door and Window store. (Photograph courtesy of Tony Russomanno.)

This view from the 1940s shows the headquarters of The Seeing Eye, the famous school that provides guide dogs for the blind. The Seeing Eye was started in 1929 by Dorothy Harrison Eustisis, who purchased the Whippany Road estate of Robert McEwan in 1931. In 1965 the school relocated to new quarters in Morristown. The McEwan estate was razed when the property was acquired by Bell Labs. (Photograph courtesy of The Seeing Eye.)

A group of students at the Whippany headquarters of The Seeing Eye takes a practice walk with the dogs in this early 1950s scene. In the 34 years that The Seeing Eye was located in Whippany, more than 4,600 dogs were trained and matched with nearly 3,000 blind persons. (Photograph courtesy of The Seeing Eye.)

Taking a break from the training routine, students and their guide dogs gather around the patio of The Seeing Eye's headquarters on Whippany Road in the 1950s. Blind people came here from all over the world to learn to use the dogs and live more independent lives. No doubt many of these people have special memories of their time at the old McEwan estate. (Photograph courtesy of The Seeing Eye.)

Trainees at The Seeing Eye in the 1950s share a meal together at the Whippany headquarters, their canine companions at their sides. The Seeing Eye's mission is to help blind people achieve greater independence, dignity, and self-confidence through the use of guide dogs. Now relocated to Morristown, The Seeing Eye continues its outstanding philanthropic work started so long ago in Whippany. (Photograph courtesy of The Seeing Eye.)

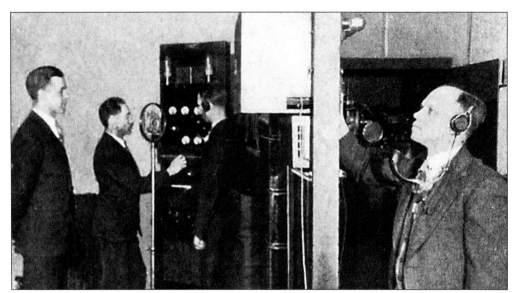

Bell Telephone Laboratories started in Whippany in 1926 with the purchase of land and buildings from Richard H. McEwan. It located its fledgling research facility in a former cow barn and on April 2, 1927, the first television broadcast in history was transmitted from Whippany. In this photograph from the Lucent Archives, a group of performers are shown speaking and singing their parts as that historic first broadcast was made. (Photograph courtesy of Lucent Archives Collection.)

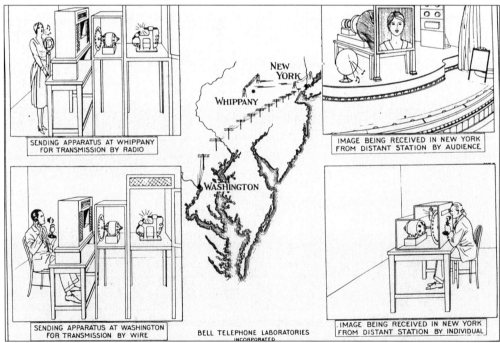

Within the Lucent Archives Collection is this sketch that shows how history's first television broadcast on April 2, 1927, was transmitted from Whippany, New Jersey, and Washington, D.C., to receiving audiences in New York City. (Photograph courtesy of Lucent Archives Collection.)

Bell Labs is seen from the employee parking lot in the 1950s. The main work here has always been focused on the needs of the military, but in the post-war period the company contributed considerably to the advances in telephone and computer technology that we enjoy today. A leader in its field, Bell Labs is now a major component of Lucent Technology. (Photograph courtesy of Lucent Archives Collection.)

Bell Labs workers are shown in this 1950s photograph unloading an Air Force cargo DC-3 at Morristown Municipal Airport. The Whippany facility contributed immeasurably to the successful development of radar during World War II, sophisticated guidance systems for ballistic missiles during the Cold War, and the design of communications satellites in the 1960s. Today Bell Labs continues its research in the fields of telecommunications and computer programming. (Photograph courtesy of Morristown Municipal Airport.)

A crowd estimated at between 5,000 and 10,000 people jammed the Morristown Municipal Airport on May 20, 1956, to witness the annual Air Fair. Some of the featured displays at the airport, which is completely within the confines of Hanover Township, were put on by various aviation firms in Morris County, at that time a leader in research of aircraft radio and control instruments. (Photograph courtesy Morristown Municipal Airport.)

The Airport Committee of the Morristown Area Chamber of Commerce, one of the sponsors of the May 20, 1956 show, termed the event an "outstanding success." Pictured here is one of that group's publicity photographs. (Photograph courtesy of Morristown Municipal Airport.)

Nearly every type of aircraft was either on display at the field on May 20, 1956—including this Air Force DC-3—or flew overhead during the Air Fair. A formation of seven Air Force jets performed a fly-by, as did a Navy blimp from the Lakehurst Naval Air Station. A NIKE guided missile was on display and the National Guard exhibited self-propelled Howitzers. (Photograph courtesy of Morristown Municipal Airport.)

Several manufacturers had new private planes on display during the May 20, 1956 Air Fair. Helicopters, like this one from Whippany's Suburban Propane Gas Company, The Port Authority of New York and the U.S. Army were also at the field. By contrast, there were several antique automobiles displayed on the tarmac during the four-hour show. (Photograph courtesy of Morristown Municipal Airport.)

In late 1947 John Tibus, a well-known Chevrolet automobile dealer on Route 10 East, moved his business and opened a GMC dealership on School Street behind the Whippany firehouse. Early Hanover Township Public Works and Police Department vehicles were purchased from the Tibus dealership. (Photograph courtesy of Tony Russomanno.)

In the early part of 1954, Bill Fritze moved his business from a smaller building in the township to the old Tibus building on School Street. Installing heat and air conditioning systems for over 50 years, Fritze and Sons presently does business from this location. (Photograph courtesy of Tony Russomanno.)

William Michas started his first food store on Ridgedale Avenue in 1920. Later his sons Harry and George opened this larger store across the street in 1955. This site today houses a liquor store and deli. Presently, the Michas family continues to serve the community from two other locations in Hanover Township. (Photograph courtesy of Tony Russomanno.)

The popular local trucking outfit for the paper mills was Cardinale, which was located on Route 10 East in the building that now serves J.R. Tobacco. Pictured here on June 18, 1955, is a 1945 White tractor ready to pick up another load of rolled paper. With its distinctive Cardinal logo, the slogan on the truck reminded everyone to "Ship the RED BIRD Route." (Photograph courtesy of Tony Russomanno.)

In 1921 the Manhattan Rubber Company established its manufacturing plant in Cedar Knolls on Townsend Avenue. In 1935 the Flintkote Company built its new plant and took over the operations of Manhattan Rubber. Flintkote added a research lab (seen here in the early 1960s) in 1946. Flintkote was a leading firm in the manufacture of liquid asphalt and coatings used in construction work. (Photograph courtesy of Morristown & Erie Railway.)

This building, home of Morristown Lumber and Supply's Whippany Branch, remains standing presently as Comfort Heating and Air Conditioning, just west of the railroad crossing on Route 10. The locals could purchase lumber and other building materials from Morristown Lumber. This c. 1950s photograph still shows a three-lane highway passing through town. (Photograph courtesy of Tony Russomanno.)

Four
Churches and Schools

In 1853 the cornerstone of the little white chapel was laid for Our Lady of Mercy in Whippany. The priests from nearby Madison served the Whippany parish until 1881. At that point OLM came to be served by Morristown clergy. In July 1883, Rev. James Brennan was assigned as the first resident pastor. This bucolic view of the OLM Chapel was taken on October 2, 1962. (Photograph courtesy of Tony Russomanno.)

The Our Lady of Mercy School opened for pre-kindergarten to fifth-grade classes in 1954. Today the school remains with a new parish hall addition in the rear of the building. (Photograph courtesy of Tony Russomanno.)

This home on Whippany Road next to the Our Lady of Mercy Chapel, shown c. 1950s, once acted as the convent for the parish. The building still remains today and houses the caretaker for the church and school and his family. (Photograph courtesy of Tony Russomanno.)

This scene of the Our Lady of Mercy Church, built in 1954, shows the altar and pews soon after the church's opening. Today parishioners find a completely remodeled interior when attending mass. (Photograph courtesy of Tony Russomanno.)

The Our Lady of Mercy Quonset hut, opened on April 18, 1949, boasted a spacious interior. In addition to school activities, community functions and formal affairs were often held here. (Photograph courtesy of Tony Russomanno.)

Pictured here in 1957 is the second St. John's Ukrainian Catholic Church, built in 1950. The church stands unaltered today on the corner of Route 10 East and South Jefferson Road. The congregation quickly outgrew the original 1922 building, which is now the parish hall. (Photograph courtesy of Tony Russomanno.)

This scene of the faithful gathered around the altar of St. John's Ukrainian Church during Christmas 1952 represents a far cry from the days when the Ukrainian priests had to celebrate mass outdoors and hold confession under the trees before their first church was erected in 1922. The present church, located at the corner of South Jefferson Road and Route 10 East, was built in 1950. (Photograph courtesy of Tony Russomanno.)

56

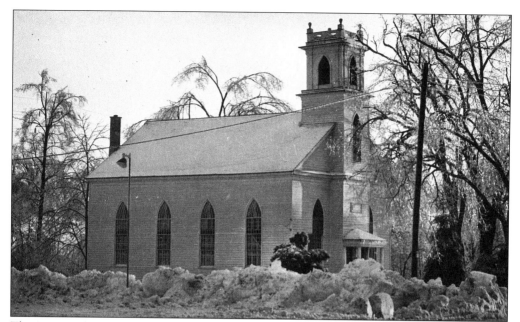

The First Presbyterian Church of Whippany was completed on July 16, 1834. The Rev. W.W. Newell was the first pastor. This photograph taken in February 1962 shows the church standing at Route 10 West before any alterations had taken place. (Photograph courtesy of Tony Russomanno.)

M.E. Church, Whippany, N.J.

The Methodist church, built around 1825, was once located at Route 10 West and Troy Hills Road. During the 1850s the church was completely overhauled and repainted, but due to a dwindling membership the church was razed in the early 1930s. (Photograph courtesy of the collection of R.F. Krygoski.)

In the early 1890s the Monroe Union Chapel was erected on Whippany Road near Park Avenue. Replacing a much smaller church and hall, this chapel served the Methodists in the township for many years. Today the chapel still stands as a center for the township's senior citizens. (Photograph courtesy of Hanover Township Landmark Committee.)

The Hilldale Park Presbyterian Church on Ridgedale Avenue in Cedar Knolls still stands today. The original building, a portable structure purchased from Sears Roebuck & Company, was set up on property donated by Mr. Hild. As the congregation grew, a larger chapel was needed. On May 30, 1942, the cornerstone was set, but several more years went by before the building was complete. (Photograph courtesy of Hilldale Park Presbyterian Church.)

The original Whippany School, built sometime in the 1790s, occupied the same property as the Presbyterian church. It comprised two educational departments that ensured an "adequate means of secular instruction." This photograph was taken sometime in the 1890s when the wooden school was approximately 100 years old. In 1909 it was condemned and a new Whippany School was opened in 1913. (Photograph courtesy of Hanover Township Landmark Committee.)

After a prolonged dispute, school trustees agreed to build a new facility on the hill site. Concern for children crossing the railroad tracks to access the school was a problem. At that time the only road to the property was School Street. In 1913 the school opened as a four-classroom facility. Presently, the building is owned by the Calais School for Children. (Photograph courtesy of Hanover Township Landmark Committee.)

This photograph from the early 1900s shows a classroom in the new Whippany School. Pupils came from other parts of the township such as Morris Plains, Parsippany, and Troy Hills. Superintendent J. Howard Hutsart at the time called it "the best four room schoolhouse in New Jersey." (Photograph courtesy of Hanover Township Landmark Committee.)

Monroe School, built in 1876, was used for Sunday school and church for the local Methodists. Once the membership outgrew this building, a new church and hall were built just to the south on Whippany Road. This photograph was taken c. 1954, a few years before the building's demolition. (Photograph courtesy of Hanover Township Landmark Committee.)

The students at the Fordville Private School on Ford Hill Road gathered for a class portrait on a frosty winter day *c.* 1890. The school was run by Sarah Elizabeth Ford; children from Hanover and neighboring communities went to classes and slept here during the week. (Photograph courtesy of Hanover Township Landmark Committee.)

The Cedar Knolls School was constructed in 1928 to replace a portable elementary school that was usually located in the Malapardis section. The Cedar Knolls School was recently sold and is now known as the Allegro School, a private educational facility for autistic children. (Photograph courtesy of Hanover Township Landmark Committee.)

Accordion players Florence, Irene, and Pauline take center stage during band practice at Cedar Knolls School in the mid 1950s. The boys in the background are all playing various wind instruments. (Photograph courtesy of Tony Russomanno.)

The Whippany School auditorium, later added to the original four-classroom school, was the popular spot for plays and dance recitals. Seen here in the 1950s are children performing for their family and friends in one of many productions at the school. (Photograph courtesy of Tony Russomanno.)

Five

"Whippany Makes Paper; Paper Makes Whippany"

The famous Eden Mill was originally known in 1844 as the Phoenix Mill. In 1853 the beginnings of the first Eden Mill were constructed, but in 1857 the mill failed. Daniel Coghlan purchased the mill in 1861. The outbreak of the Civil War caused paper prices to skyrocket and Eden became very profitable. Diamond Paper Mills purchased Eden in 1884 and for a time it was known as "The Diamond." (Photograph courtesy of Hanover Township Landmark Committee.)

Robert McEwan was born in Scotland in 1828 and emigrated to America while still in his early twenties. In 1890 this man, along with his seven sons, created the beginnings of a family paper dynasty in Whippany. The McEwan Brothers' Company eventually grew to become one of the largest paper concerns in the east. (Photograph courtesy of Mrs. Richard W. McEwan Jr.)

United Box Board Mill, Whippany, N. J.

This early 1900s postcard view looks west and shows the site of the early Eden Mill complex along the main line of the Morristown & Erie Railroad. The train seen in the picture is headed back to Morristown. The stone embankments for the Eden Mill Lane overpass seen to the right of the image remain today, but the road has been long abandoned. (Photograph courtesy of the collection of Steven Hepler.)

281. Residence of R. J. Coughlan, showing Caledonian Mill., Whippany, N. J.

In 1842 the Caledonian Mill (seen here in a 1900 postcard view) was constructed. Daniel Coghlan operated this mill until the mid-1890s, when it was purchased by Robert McEwan. For several decades it operated under the McEwan banner until becoming home to the International Paper Company. Today the refurbished mill building is the site of Corporate Communications Group on Parsippany Road in Whippany. (Photograph courtesy of the collection of Steven Hepler.)

Hanover Mill started as a cotton mill on the Whippany River in 1830. Robert McEwan acquired this mill in the mid-1890s along with Eden, Caledonian, and Stony Brook Mills. In 1933 the Desiderio Brothers purchased Hanover Mill and established the Whippany Paper Board Company. Today the mill has been converted into a multi-commercial business park. (Photograph courtesy of John Durkota.)

Arthur McEwan managed the Eden Mill complex and was considered by the employees to be a congenial and fun-loving man. When his brother Richard died in 1936, Arthur assumed the presidency of the Morristown & Erie Railroad. When Arthur passed away in April 1943, he was the last McEwan brother to be associated with the Whippany mills. (Photograph courtesy of Mrs. Richard W. McEwan Jr.)

The Stony Brook Mill at Malapardis is seen in an early-1950s view. The original mill was acquired by the McEwan brothers in the late 1890s and became their principal box-making facility. In 1945 Stony Brook was purchased by the Desiderio Brothers' Whippany Paper Board Company. The mill was demolished in the early 1980s. (Photograph courtesy of Tony Russomanno.)

With their 1945 purchase of the McEwan mills, the seven Desiderio Brothers managed Whippany Paper Board, a $50-million industrial empire and the country's largest manufacturer of paperboard. Anthony, president of the firm, is seated at the desk. From left to right are brothers Dominick, John, Thomas, Arnold, Salvatore, and Michael. (Photograph courtesy of Hanover Township Landmark Committee.)

This aerial view depicts Whippany Paper Board's giant Eden Mill complex after it was enlarged in 1958 at a cost of $24 million. By 1959 the plant was in full operation with a daily capacity of nearly 1,000 tons of paperboard. The shipping room at Eden was large enough to house 20 railroad cars and 29 trailer trucks together under one roof. (Photograph courtesy of Hanover Township Landmark Committee.)

John Durkota, pictured here in his office on March 8, 1941, was the personnel manager of the Eden Mill plant. John liked to take photographs in his spare time and we have him to thank for all the scarce interior photographs of workmen at the plant. (Photograph courtesy of John Durkota.)

At the Eden Mill plant in 1941 from left to right are John Coolack, Tony Montnak, Bob Phelps, Mike Yuhas, Bob Maher, Pat Pillion, and Fred Johnson. Behind the men is the "lining machine," a piece of machinery that aligned sheets of paperboard by manual feed. (Photograph courtesy of John Durkota.)

In the early years, the Eden Mill plant had two operating paper machines (numbers 1 and 2). Seen here at the "dry end" of number 2 on March 7, 1941, are, from left to right, as follows: (kneeling) Tom Ryan, Al Zega, and an unidentified man; (standing) Joe De Lukey, Jim Ryan, Tony Chayka, Alfred Ellis, and Tony Mihalko. (Photograph courtesy of John Durkota.)

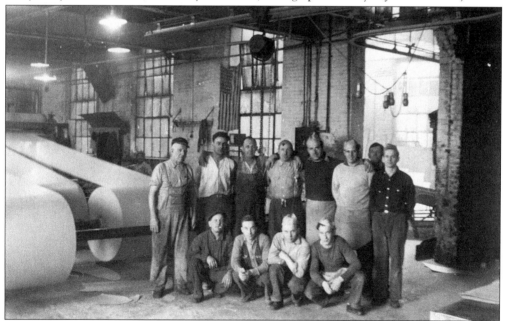

At the end of the paper-making machine the finished product would come out onto a roll and then had to be rewound, and thus this was called the "rewind department." From left to right c. 1941 are as follows: (kneeling) Patzy Lanza, Jack McGill, Andy Woytas, and Joe Coolack; (standing) Joe White, Tom Adamsky, Bill Lockwood, Paul Boba, Frank Cherowitz, Frank Valante, unidentified, and Tony Coolack. (Photograph courtesy of John Durkota.)

This c. 1941 photograph shows John Durkota (left) and Chris Waishes (master mechanic) on the roof of Eden Mill next to the shift whistle. This whistle in the earlier years would be blown at 7 a.m. and 5 p.m., letting workmen know their shift was ending or beginning. If the whistle sounded a steady blast, this meant there was a fire on the mill property. (Photograph courtesy of John Durkota.)

The "oil men"—two of Eden Mill's maintenance mechanics—fill their oil cans in the shop during their shift. It was a never-ending job to keep all moving parts in this large plant well lubricated and problem-free. On the left is Joe "Oily Joe" Kuzminsky and on the right is Tony Bolcar. (Photograph courtesy of John Durkota.)

With the paper industry growing daily, the McEwan Brothers in later years had to add two more paper-making machines, numbers 3 and 4. This *c.* 1941 photograph shows Bill Lockweed on the left and Joe White near the "wet end" of number one. (Photograph courtesy of John Durkota.)

Frank Giblock on the left and Bill Lockwood are seen here near the "wet end" of number 2 on March 7, 1941. In this photograph you can get an idea of just how long a paper-making machine can be. Note the many large, steam-filled steel rollers that the paper must pass through to dry. (Photograph courtesy of John Durkota.)

The McEwan Brothers' shipping department at Eden Mill was a beehive of activity on a cold day in the winter of 1940. John Durkota had his camera and photographed the workers as they paused from shoveling snow away from the loading docks. M & E No. 6 switches cars in the background. About this time No. 6 had been outfitted with steam jets to melt snow and ice away from the track switches.

Bill Metzger—pictured here on March 7, 1941—was one of the powerhouse's chief engineers. Steam plays a big part in the paper-making process. The steam is produced in high-pressure boilers, and then it travels through pipes to the steel rollers of the paper machines for the purpose of drying the wet product. (Photograph courtesy of John Durkota.)

Andy Kowchak, seen here *c.* 1941 standing next to one of the McEwan Brothers' trucks, would transport loads of "chess" to one of two local landfills. Local children would often be found at these sites waiting for Andy to unload. Then they would sift through to find treasures such as coins, jewelry, and other valuables. Photograph courtesy of John Durkota.)

In every large company there is staff to perform such duties as bookkeeping and other clerical tasks. Standing outside the McEwan Brothers' Eden Mill office are, from left to right, Mary Cherry, John McEwan, and Pierce Welsh. This photograph was taken on November 26, 1942. (Photograph courtesy of John Durkota.)

This is a 1960s view of the International Paper Company on Parsippany Road. Hanover's first paper mill was built here in 1791. The Caledonian Mill was erected on this site in 1842. In 1920, Caledonian burned and a new plant run by Calvin Agar was constructed. In 1941, International Paper purchased the facility and corrugated containers were manufactured here until the late 1970s. Corporate Communications Group occupies the site today. (Photograph courtesy of Tony Russomanno.)

Only one shift was lost at the International Paper Company when its main boiler broke down at 3 p.m. on November 5, 1968. Morris County Central excursion locomotives No.'s 4039 and 385 were moved to a siding and piped up to deliver more than 16,000 pounds of steam to the mill. (Photograph courtesy of the collection of Steven Hepler.)

Six
Morristown &
Erie Railroad

In the center of modern-day Whippany stands the elegant, turn-of-the-century fieldstone passenger station of the Morristown & Erie Railroad, shown here in the mid-1950s. Erected in 1904 and officially opened on Friday, January 7, 1905, the depot additionally served as the general office of the railroad. Today, this historic structure is still owned by the M & E and functions as the office of Alice Slattery Real Estate. (Photograph courtesy of Homer R. Hill.)

This late-1930s view features the rear of the Morristown & Erie's Whippany passenger station and general office, freight house, and water tank. The M & E operated frequent local passenger service between Morristown, Whippany, and Essex Fells from November 21, 1904, until April 28, 1928. Additionally, a through-train service to Jersey City and Manhattan was provided via an Erie Railroad connection at Essex Fells. (Photograph courtesy of Donald Van Court.)

This mid-1950s view shows the M & E's Whippany freight house (now home of the Whippany Railway Museum) while it was still at its original location just west of the water tank on the station side of the tracks. The building is some 20 feet longer in this view than it is today. The 1904 structure was moved to its present site across the tracks from the passenger depot in 1967. (Photograph courtesy of Collection of Steven Hepler.)

In 1895 construction began on the 4-mile Whippany River Railroad (WR), the forerunner of today's Morristown & Erie. The WR had only one locomotive for its passenger service. The locomotive was originally a Pennsylvania Railroad engine built in the 1870s. When it arrived on the WR it was given the road number "1" and named "WHIPPANY." The WHIPPANY is seen here near its namesake town c. 1898. (Photograph courtesy of Hanover Township Landmark Committee.)

This photograph shows the first commuter ticket issued for the Whippany River Railroad by Superintendent John Melick on December 4, 1895, the first day of passenger service on the 4-mile WR. Freight service to the paper mills in Whippany had commenced several months prior on August 16, 1895. The actual ticket still exists and is in the archives of the Hanover Township Landmark Committee. (Photograph courtesy of the collection of Steven Hepler.)

The M & E No. 2 and train are seen near Whippany about 1915. This diminutive locomotive was built in 1894 for the Chicago South Side Elevated Railroad. It was acquired by the M & E in 1908 and placed into passenger service. Loved by passengers and crew, it was nicknamed "The Dinky." In 1922 No. 2 was sold to the Hanover Brick company, where it worked until the brick works closed in 1931. (Photograph courtesy of the collection of Steven Hepler.)

M & E No. 6 leaves the Whippany yard on May 11, 1942, and is about to back across the Newark & Mount Pleasant Turnpike (Route 10) with a trainload of empty coal hoppers bound for interchange with the Lackawanna Railroad in Morristown. No. 6, built in 1898, was a favorite locomotive among M & E crews. (Photograph courtesy of Donald Van Court.)

M & E No. 9 hustles a string of coal-laden hopper cars past the McEwan Brothers' Eden Mill on March 8, 1940. No. 9 was built in 1904 and was acquired by the M & E in October 1927. By all accounts No. 9 was a good, reliable freight engine for 17 years. She was finally scrapped in January 1947. (Photograph courtesy of John Durkota.)

Morristown & Erie 2-8-0 No. 10 crosses the Newark & Mount Pleasant Turnpike on November 27, 1946. Note the classic and long-gone "Hy-Way Diner" in the background. Today the Il Capriccio Ristorante occupies this site. No. 10 was built in 1909 and was purchased by the M & E in August 1944. She was sold for scrap in October 1955. (Photograph courtesy of Donald Van Court.)

Morristown & Erie 2-8-0 No. 11 backs away from the water tank and freight house at Whippany on Christmas Eve, 1946. The train will drift across the Newark & Mount Pleasant Turnpike and deliver a cut of cars to the McEwan Brothers' paper mills. The crew is anxious to finish up the day's work and return home to their families for the holidays. (Photograph courtesy of Donald Van Court.)

Having just crossed Route 10, Morristown & Erie No. 12 enters the Whippany yard to switch a cut of cars containing coal and paper goods for the mills in 1951. Conductor Henry (Heinie) Keys rides the footboards. No. 12 was acquired in June 1946 and ended her operating days along with Nos. 10 and 11 with the arrival of diesel switcher No. 14 in April 1952. (Photograph courtesy of Homer R. Hill.)

"Heinie" Keys stands on the platform of the M & E "bobber" caboose No. 1 at Whippany on February 17, 1940. This unique, four-wheel caboose, built in the 1890s by the Lackawanna Railroad, was acquired by the M & E in 1933. It was used at the rear end of all freights until 1950. The caboose survives today and may return to the Whippany Railway Museum in 1998. (Photograph courtesy of John Durkota.)

Railbus No. 10 was built by the White Motor Company in 1918 for the M & E's local passenger service. In this photograph, No. 10 is at Whippany in 1921 sitting on the specially built turntable that was located a few yards east of the fieldstone depot. Today the bus is preserved by the Whippany Railway Museum and is a unique example of New Jersey transportation history. (Photograph courtesy of Whippany Railway Museum Collection.)

A Morristown & Erie section gang and motor car No. 4 are at Thomas Street (Parsippany Road) in Whippany on February 25, 1943. The crew is heading up the now abandoned line to the C.A. Agar Co. (present-day Corporate Communications Group) and Hanover Mill (present-day 9 Whippany Road). From left to right are John Farrinhotto, Joe Dandino, and Frank Studley. (Photograph courtesy of Donald Van Court.)

M & E No. 12 takes on water at Whippany while pulling a special excursion on September 20, 1947, 19 years after the railroad discontinued all passenger service. The coaches behind the locomotive were borrowed from the Erie Railroad for the day. The M & E displayed its equipment for the benefit of excursionists and mementos of the bygone passenger days were handed out. (Photograph courtesy of Railroad Avenue Enterprises Collection, R.H. Young photograph.)

The M & E No. 14 arrives at Whippany on its first trip on April 28, 1952. Standing in front of the engine, from left to right, are Henry Becker, Phil Dahil, Mauritius Jensen, R.W. McEwan Jr., Joe Dandino, Tommy Gee, Howard Roff, Kenneth Jones, Frank Studley, and Fletcher Williams. The locomotive was named in honor of Mr. Jensen, who had been with the M & E for 50 years. (Photograph courtesy of Whippany Railway Museum Collection.)

Morristown & Erie No. 15 was purchased from the U.S. Navy in October 1963 as a standby for No. 14. Upon arrival at the M & E, it was painted in the same scheme as 14 and named for former company president R.W. McEwan Jr. In this scene No. 15 crosses Parsippany Road in Whippany and heads west back to Morristown on February 18, 1965. (Photograph courtesy of Bob Pennisi.)

After a 13-year absence, steam locomotives returned to the M & E in 1965 when the Morris County Central Railroad (MCC) began operating seasonal excursion trains. A creation of Parsippany resident Earle Gil, the MCC proved to be very popular during its 1965–73 period on the M & E. Here, 1907 engine No. 385 is headed east over the School Street bridge. Whippany School on Highland Avenue appears in the background. (Photograph courtesy of E.H. Brown.)

MCC engine No. 4039 is seen teamed up with No. 385 at Whippany prior to the start of a special excursion to Essex Fells in November 1967. Built in 1942, No. 4039 was added to the MCC roster late in 1965. Currently owned by the Whippany Railway Museum, this engine is awaiting restoration and a return to active service in Hanover Township. (Photograph courtesy of the collection of Steven Hepler.)

Seven
Township Services

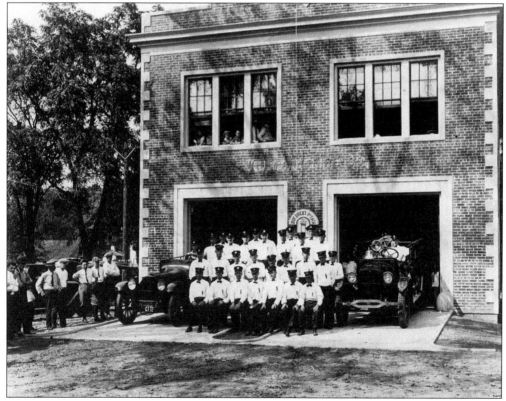

Through donations and fund-raisers—"Buy Bricks, $1.00 each"—the Whippany Firehouse was completed in 1923. It has two large truck bays, a meeting room, and a large hall on the second floor. (Photograph courtesy of Hanover Township Landmark Committee.)

Seen here in the late 1920s are members of the Whippany Fire Department sporting their new fire gear and equipment. Even though flashlights were available in the 1920s, you can see the old kerosene type lanterns hanging on the sides of the trucks in front of the drivers. (Photograph courtesy of Hanover Township Landmark Committee.)

Whippany's bravest were brought together for this mid-1950s photograph. In 1958 the department added an addition to the right side of the building to house their newest piece of equipment, a 1958 Mack pumper. Today the completely restored '58 Mack is used for parades and special functions. (Photograph courtesy of Whippany Fire Company.)

In the 1950s and 1960s it wasn't strange to see someone sitting out in front of the firehouse watching cars go by. Sitting and enjoying a quiet Sunday on the left is John Yavorski; on the right is Edward Guerin. This photograph also shows how the flagpole was once mounted on the roof of the building. (Photograph courtesy of Tony Russomanno.)

One of Whippany Fire Department's finest pieces of machinery was the 1935 Seagrave. The truck had a V-12 engine and could pump 1,250 gallons of water per minute. When the Seagrave was delivered it came via a railroad flat car and was unloaded at the Whippany railroad depot. (Photograph courtesy of the collection of R.F. Krygoski.)

The apparatus shown here are, from left to right, a 1939 GMC pumper, a 1948 GMC utility truck, and a 1935 Seagrave pumper. You may notice that there are three vehicles but only two garage doors. Back then traffic wasn't a problem; getting out of the building was the hard part. (Photograph courtesy of Tony Russomanno.)

From this photograph we can see how, in the early years, firemen would brave the heat and smoke without gloves and with rubber coats and leather helmets. Fighting fires was quite a task. Today's equipment makes fire-fighting safer, but it's still dangerous. (Photograph courtesy of Tony Russomanno.)

In 1942 the First Aid Squad in Hanover Township was formed by the Cedar Knolls Fire Department. An old hearse was purchased from Lanterman & Hughson funeral directors in Morristown for $200 with contributions solicited by firemen. Today the department continues to provide emergency medical care for the entire township. (Photograph courtesy of Eugene Clemens.)

The dedication ceremonies for the Cedar Knolls Firehouse were held on June 25, 1938. This three-story building complete with two bowling lanes, a community hall, and meeting and training rooms proved to be very spacious in its day. To accommodate the growing community and larger apparatus, the fire department built two additions to this original structure. A 1956 Cadillac ambulance and 1966 Mack pumper are parked out front. (Photograph courtesy of Hanover Township Landmark Committee.)

The "Burning of the Mortgage" ceremony on June 6, 1954, was a great occasion for the members of the Cedar Knolls Fire Department. With township officials and the public watching, department officials Chief Robert Herudek, Fire Company President Joseph A. Bishop, and Fire Commissioner Leo L. Halko did the honors. (Photograph courtesy of Tony Russomanno.)

After the mortgage-burning, two of the department's earliest members unveiled a memorial plaque. On the left is Samuel Johnson and assisting is Michael Beresh. The memorial plaque is dedicated to "All Who Have Served the Department Well." (Photograph courtesy of Tony Russomanno.)

The fire department purchased this 1945 Mack during World War II. At $9,000, the unit was delivered with no chrome fixtures because of the war effort. Also parked in front is the department's second 1953 Cadillac ambulance. (Photograph courtesy of Tony Russomanno.)

Soon after the Cedar Knolls firehouse was completed in 1938, members lined up for a group photograph. Showing both young and older members, this photograph was possibly taken after a Memorial Day parade. (Photograph courtesy of Tony Russomanno.)

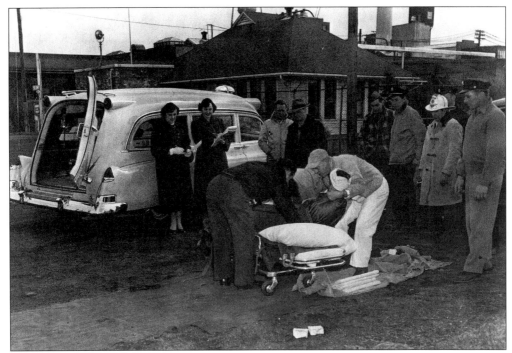

At one of the town's local mills, first aid squad and fire department members staged a mock incident. The injured were treated and prepared to be transported. First aider Bob Herudek helps load a patient onto the stretcher while Whippany Fire Chief Ted Guerin (in the white helmet) looks on. (Photograph courtesy of Tony Russomanno.)

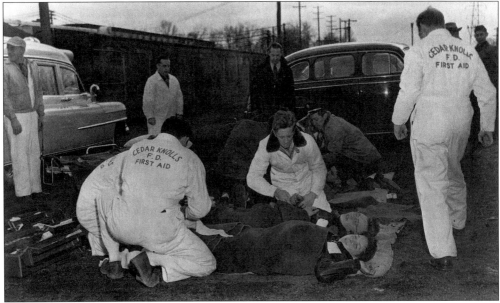

The volunteers shown here spend many hours training and also attend Red Cross first aid classes. Today's first aid volunteers (EMTs) are required to be certified by the state. This certification mandates over 100 hours of classroom training in addition to hospital emergency room training. (Photograph courtesy of Tony Russomanno.)

Standing to the left on the apron of the Whippany firehouse is Eugene F. Clemens Jr., who was appointed to the position of chief in 1936. At 22 years of age he was considered the youngest police chief in the United States. Lieutenant Bill Meeker on the right was brought onto the force in 1938. Also seen here are two of the township's earlier patrol vehicles. (Photograph courtesy of Tony Russomanno.)

Captain John W. Cortwright—standing in the center—was the second full-time officer brought onto the force in 1937. Pictured with John are special police officers. These men would volunteer their time patrolling the township with full-time officers. They would also work at events directing traffic and controlling crowds. (Photograph courtesy of Tony Russomanno.)

In 1961 this fine group of special police officers was also sworn in to help out the regular officers in their free time. Pictured from left to right are Emil D. Knad, Val Yesenko, John Hundley, James T. Growley, and Al Behrens. (Photograph courtesy of Tony Russomanno.)

Hanover Township Police Chief Eugene Clemens and an unknown patrolman are standing behind the 1938 Model 80 Harley Davidson motorcycle. The location of this photograph was in the parking lot of the Esso gas station on Route 10 East, once situated just east of the present Route 287 overpass. The station was later removed for the Route 287 North off-ramp. (Photograph courtesy of Eugene F. Clemens, Jr.

In 1946 after he returned from the war, Ted Guerin was appointed superintendent of the department of roads for the township. Ted is seen here next to the first new pick-up truck, an early-1950s GMC. With only a few full-timers and limited equipment, the department managed to keep the town in great shape. (Photograph courtesy of Tony Russomanno.)

The township's first garbage truck—shown here on August 27, 1947—was purchased new from the Tibus dealership on School Street in Whippany. In the days before recycling, trash would be thrown in the rear of the vehicle and then taken to local dumps for disposal. (Photograph courtesy of Tony Russomanno.)

Hanover Township Mayor Anthony Ferraiuolo (on the ladder) and Ted Guerin, superintendent of roads, installed one of the town's first official street signs in 1951. School Street, located next to the Whippany firehouse, was at one time the only road that led to Whippany School, passing under the railroad tracks and up the hill. (Photograph courtesy of Tony Russomanno.)

With the department of public works growing in the early 1950s, the agency needed property to store equipment and materials. Edward A. Guerin, Ted Guerin's father, worked out an agreement with the town to use his property behind 468 Route 10 as a site for a garage. In 1965 the department was moved to its present facility on North Jefferson Road. (Photograph courtesy of Tony Russomanno.).

Eight
Community Activities

Sponsored by the Whippany Fire Company, the champs seen above are, from left to right, as follows: (sitting) Andy Belusko, Toby Kaviack, Dick Japko, Bob Kasiski, Mike Yavorski, John Habuda, Bucky Chapman, Jim Mulcahey, and Jack Kasiski; (standing) John Kasiski, Larry Chemeloicz, Joe Kehoe, Bill Kehoe, Moose Kiely, ? Grumpka, Ed Sherman, Tony Yavorski, and Andy Durma. Batboy Walter Boyer is on the ground. (Photograph courtesy of Tony Russomanno.)

This baseball team, sponsored in the 1950s by the Braviak Funeral Home, relaxes after a game. Often players from other towns would join the team, making it difficult for us to identify each member. Look closely as you may be in this photograph. (Photograph courtesy of Tony Russomanno.)

At the ball field on Route 10 West, the present-day site of the Jefferson Road jughandle, is the Malapardis team. In the background one can see the smokestack from McEwan Brothers' Stony Brook paper mill. Just west of the ball field stood the Malapardis School, which in the mid-1950s was converted into the township municipal building. (Photograph courtesy of Tony Russomanno.)

The American Legion Post 155 in Whippany sponsored the boys in the late 1950s. They are, from left to right, as follows: (sitting) Bob Kasiski, Dick Japko, Andy Durma, Peachy Kimble, and Jack Kasiski; (standing) Mike Yavorski, "Hans" Kramer, unidentified, Billy Kehoe, unidentified, unidentified, and John Habuda. (Photograph courtesy of Tony Russomanno.)

How many residents recall the days when local teams would play baseball in the shadow of the Stony Brook Mill's 175-foot-tall smokestack? This ball field, home to Hanover teams, was positioned where the Jefferson Road jughandle is now located. Today, everything in this photograph is but a memory. (Photograph courtesy of Tony Russomanno.)

These six lovely young ladies have just participated in a mid-1950s swimming contest at Anchor Swim Club and they are proudly showing off the trophies they won. A happy occasion indeed, but we keep wondering what the significance is of the "bunny ears" and whisker make-up the girls are wearing. (Photograph courtesy of Tony Russomanno.)

A diver is seen in action during a contest at the Anchor Swim Club in 1958. The crowd has gathered poolside to watch the participants vie for first prize. This pool was located on Route 10 East adjacent to DeMaio's Restaurant. Today the pool lies abandoned, a victim of rapidly changing times. (Photograph courtesy of Tony Russomanno.)

A large group of children gathers for the photographer during a "learn-to-swim" class at Anchor Swim Club on July 19, 1956. Most youth swimming classes throughout New Jersey were sponsored by local Red Cross affiliates. Today, trucks and cars roar by overhead on Route 287, oblivious to the deserted pool and the ghosts of long-forgotten summers that haunt this site. (Photograph courtesy of Tony Russomanno.)

What would a day at the swim club be in the summer of 1957 without a watermelon-eating contest? A group of boys are quickly devouring the tasty melons in a race to see who can finish first. Our bets are on the young man in the striped trunks, second from left. He's nearly finished and everyone else has barely started. Next is the hot dog eating event. (Photograph courtesy of Tony Russomanno.)

The Whippany Boys' Club was organized by the members seen here in this late-1940s photograph. From left to right they are as follows: (kneeling) Ed "Twinkle Toes" Dolbear, Dick Japko, Jack Kasiski, Jake "Kuba" Lopata, and Frank Kasisky; (standing) Bob "Kas" Kasiski, Tony "Antek" Yavorski, Ed "Big Mack" Makowski, Mike "Yeja Boat" Yavorski, Mike "Izzy" Sagarese, and Frank "Hooks" Krygoski. (Photograph courtesy of Tony Russomanno.)

The Whippany Industrial Bowling League team seen here on May 25, 1961, was sponsored by Sanchelli Trucking. From left to right are Wally Ruddela, Paul Pilipie, Joe Sanchelli, Art Fisher, and Vick Vreeland. (Photograph courtesy of Tony Russomanno.)

The Veterans of Foreign Wars (VFW) Post 5351 in Whippany completed construction of its headquarters in 1956. Very active in many youth-related programs in the township, the veterans took over the annual Christmas Tree Program after World War II. The traditions of handing out stockings and lighting the Christmas tree were originally started by Mrs. Arthur McEwan over 50 years ago and are carried on by the veterans today. (Photograph courtesy of Tony Russomanno.)

Here members of the Veterans of Foreign Wars Post 5351 raise money at a carnival booth to support their organization. The gentlemen pictured are Lou Dombrowski (left) and Frank Minerowicz. The young lady is unidentified. (Photograph courtesy of Tony Russomanno.)

The American Legion Post 155 in Whippany was organized on May 25, 1926. In 1957, property on Eden Mill Lane (now Legion Place) was acquired and the new post opened on October 19, 1957. Pictured from left to right are John Korn, John Sharry, Ed Makowski, Ed Safko, George Skurchak, John Bolcar, Dick Japko, and auxiliary member Ann Zega. The group is gathered to celebrate the burning of the mortgage. (Photograph courtesy of Tony Russomanno.)

The Sons of the American Legion Post 155 are seen here during one of their paper drives. Funds for projects and community activities were raised by dances, raffles, and rentals of the group's large hall. One of the legion's popular events is an annual Easter Egg Hunt in which all children from the township can participate. (Photograph courtesy of Tony Russomanno.)

At the Air Fair at Morristown Municipal Airport on May 20, 1956, members of the American Legion Post 155 sold raffle tickets to raise money for their organization. Proudly displaying the 1956 Chevrolet sedan are, from left to right, ? Ozinkowski, Tony Baranowski, and Pete Zailo. (Photograph courtesy of Morristown Municipal Airport.)

Seen after a Memorial Day celebration, these veterans gathered in the hall at the Whippany firehouse are, from left to right, Lou Dombrowski, Jess "Doc" Ziccarello, and Frank Minerowicz. Veterans from the American Legion and VFW sponsor the parade every year together with organizations such as the fire departments, local school bands, and clubs to honor our veterans. (Photograph courtesy of Tony Russomanno.)

At a ceremony to honor the men and women who have served their country, scouts, children, and town officials pay tribute. At the intersection of Route 10 West and Troy Hills Road stands a memorial stone that reads as follows: "Erected by the people of the Township of Hanover to perpetuate the memory of all those who have faithfully served their country." (Photograph courtesy of Tony Russomanno.)

Hanover Township servicemen stop for a photograph in front of the Whippany firehouse in 1943 during a Memorial Day service. Pictured are, from left to right, as follows: (kneeling) Mike Woytas, Joe Leana, Tony Kasiski, John Bolcar, and John Godon; (standing) unidentified, unidentified, Charley Beaumont, Jim Tighe, ? Adamsky, Bill Kanuss, John Krygoski, John Tibus, George Buce, and Wilbur Davenport. (Photograph courtesy of Tony Russomanno.)

The Whippany Rotary Club of Rotary International originated in 1948. Business owners from the township raise money from community events such as the annual Duck Race and Spaghetti Dinner. A major beneficiary is Camp Merry Heart in Hackettstown, a camp for disabled children. From left to right are members Jules Fiesinger, Bill Felts, Ted Connelly, and Dr. Raymond Dzoba, gathered to present a check to Steve Holmes (center) of Camp Merry Heart. (Photograph courtesy of Tony Russomanno.)

Veterans march down Route 10 East in this mid-1950s photograph. What's interesting here is how differently this area looks today. The men are parading down the old exit from Route 10 East to Mount Pleasant Avenue, which is now blocked off. The background is vastly changed today, as this is the site of the Pine Plaza Shopping Center. Additionally, both dwellings seen here are no longer standing. (Photograph courtesy of Tony Russomanno.)

Servicemen home on leave act as pallbearers in a *c.* 1944 funeral for one of their fallen comrades. After leaving Fagan's Funeral Home on Route 10, the procession moves east to the church. The servicemen are, from left to right, (driver's side) Jess Ziccarello, Walter Minerowicz, Bill Bolcar, and an unidentified sailor; (passenger side) Gerard Bisson. (Photograph courtesy of Tony Russomanno.)

This memorial, which honored Hanover Township men and women who served in World War II and the Korean War, stood on property of the Morristown & Erie Railroad at the Whippany station. When the railroad began to develop the site in 1967 and erected the "McEwan Building" (which today is the office of O'Toole & Couch and Gibraltar Bank), the memorial was removed and never replaced. (Photograph courtesy of Hanover Township Landmark Committee.)

Nine
"Along the Whippanong"

A favorite winter's pastime in the 1950s was to ice skate on the pond at Whippany station. The pleasant surroundings included a large duck pond, stone station, and well-kept lawns. While this was the perfect setting for an outing in any season, the railroad's development of the property in 1967 replaced the lawn and pond. (Photograph courtesy of Tony Russomanno.)

After nearly 30 years of searching, Steve Hepler (local railroad historian) was amazed when John Durkota produced this photograph he took of Morristown & Erie Engine No. 6 emerging from under the Eden Mill Lane overpass in 1940. When Eden Mill began to expand its operations, the overpass was removed and mill structures were erected to the right of the photograph. Today, the road dead-ends several yards to the left and is known as Legion Place.

The Eden Mill smokestack dominates this peaceful November 5, 1941 view of the Whippany River. To the left, one can make out the Eden Mill Lane bridge. In a month the peace would be shattered when the Japanese attack on Pearl Harbor plunged America into World War II. Throughout the war, the McEwan mills produced packing material and boxes for military supplies and ammunition. (Photograph courtesy of John Durkota.)

Vintage automobiles ply the waters of a flooded Route 10 in the aftermath of the Great Flood of 1940. The Whippany River, swelled by rainfall, had overflowed its banks and the resulting flood caused major problems along the three-lane highway where it paralleled the river. This view looks east towards East Hanover at the approximate location of the Courtyard by Marriott on Route 10 East today. (Photograph courtesy of Tony Russomanno.)

This automobile was involved in a broadside crash on Route 10, west of Jefferson Road, on July 30, 1949. Tony Russomanno was called upon by the Hanover Police Department to photograph the wreck for their investigation, a task he became all too familiar with over the years. The billboard of a young boy and his dad peering through a Ford showroom window is an ironic play on this grim scene. (Photograph courtesy of Tony Russomanno.)

These next four photographs are early 1950s views of what we like to call The Four Corners of Whippany: the intersection of Mount Pleasant Avenue and Parsippany Road. Here, as we look east down Mount Pleasant Avenue, one can see the vacant lot where the present post office would be erected in 1962. In the early-1900s, Whippanong Hall and the first post office were located on the same site. (Photograph courtesy of Tony Russomanno.)

From this position we look north up Parsippany Road and Mount Pleasant Avenue crosses from left to right. On the right side is Phil's Tavern, originally Myron Lee's Grocery and now Billy & Madeline's Red Room. (Photograph courtesy of Tony Russomanno.)

From this vantage point we look west on Mount Pleasant Avenue as the Morristown Transit jitney approaches the Parsippany Road intersection. The corner store on the left is The Union Food Store. Today, Hanover Liquors is at this location. (Photograph courtesy of Tony Russomanno.)

Finally, we are standing at the foot of Parsippany Road, looking south past the Mount Pleasant Avenue intersection. At this point Parsippany Road became Thomas Street (now Parsippany Road), which ended at Whippany Road. Just above the railroad crossing sign, in the background we can see the outline of the former home of Daniel Coghlan. (Photograph courtesy of Tony Russomanno.)

This view looks east down Route 10 from the Parsippany Road overpass after a heavy snowfall. The highway has been plowed, but only one automobile can be seen venturing out onto the roadway. Rising smoke indicates that Hanover Mill continues to contribute to Hanover Township's economy despite the unfavorable weather conditions. (Photograph courtesy of Tony Russomanno.)

This photograph is included to show the reader what Ridgedale Avenue in Cedar Knolls looked like on September 13, 1951, at the site of the Flintkote Building. This somewhat rural, two-lane country road, with an abundance of trees and very little traffic to speak of, is a far cry from the fast moving, four-lane thoroughfare of today. Oh, but to return to those quieter times! (Photograph courtesy of Tony Russomanno.)

This 1950s photograph looks south on Parsippany Road toward the Route 10 overpass. The car on the right side of the picture is turning onto Parsippany Road from Kitchell Place. The once tree-lined street is a thing of the past. (Photograph courtesy of Tony Russomanno.)

Route 10, a three-lane highway in the 1950s, was not very busy at the time of this photograph. Standing in front of the present municipal building looking west, one can see on the left side of the photograph how Malapardis Road came out to the highway. Further west on the left there once was an Esso gas station. (Photograph courtesy of Tony Russomanno.)

This photograph shows a milk truck on the three-lane Route 10 looking east from the Troy Hills Road intersection. The home on the left side of the photograph was originally located on the present site of the Whippany Diner. It was moved to make room for the highway and remains today. (Photograph courtesy of Tony Russomanno.)

The rapidly rising waters of the Whippany River flow swiftly under the Whippany Road Bridge at Route 10 during the Great Flood of 1940. The Whippany Filling Station and Mauritius Jensen's home can be seen across the highway. See pp. 111 and 117 for additional photographs. (Photograph courtesy of Hanover Township Landmark Committee.)

The large building in the center of this 1950s photograph was Grace & Ray's Tavern. The building still stands today at the intersection of Mount Pleasant Avenue and Route 10. The house in the upper left corner was razed and a small strip of stores was built in its place. (Photograph courtesy of Tony Russomanno.)

This picture taken from the entrance to the Hanover Mill is the companion photograph to the one on p. 116. It shows the First Presbyterian Church of Whippany and the fast-moving waters of the Whippany River during the Great Flood. The Whippany School can be seen on the hill overlooking the Morristown & Erie tracks in the background. (Photograph courtesy of Hanover Township Landmark Committee.)

This classic Victorian-era home at 101 Whippany Road is located on a 48-acre estate originally owned by Jesse McEwan Sr. Today the house serves as the headquarters of Crestwood Nursing Home. The manor's wraparound porch and soaring turret add a touch of elegance to this magnificent reminder of the McEwan's great influence upon the region. (Photograph courtesy of the collection of Steven Hepler.)

The home of Robert McEwan, built in 1900 and seen here c. 1913, still stands today on Parsippany Road and presently serves as the Our Lady of Mercy Rectory. In the late 1900s, McEwan moved his family to a larger home on Whippany Road. At this time Father Clifford of OLM began living in the house. There have been several changes over the years but the one original prominent point is the spire in front. (Photograph courtesy of Tony Russomanno.)

A very adventurous young man named Roxbury McCormick climbed up the inside of the smokestack of the Caladonian Mill in the early 1900s to get this aerial view of Parsippany Road (Thomas Street) intersecting with Whippany Road. The scene includes Robert McEwan's home (top center) and Arthur McEwan's home (bottom center). Both homes were built in 1900 for the paper mill owners and both homes remain today. (Photograph courtesy of Hanover Township Landmark Committee.)

This 1900s Victorian house was originally built for Arthur McEwan, who was the manager of the Eden Mill. In 1905 Arthur sold the home to Pierce Welsh. The home, located at 15 Parsippany Road, is still in the Welsh family, owned by Eugene and Betty (Welsh) Clemens. The large barn seen in the rear of the photograph has been razed. (Photograph courtesy of Betty (Welsh) Clemens.)

The 1800s home of Walter H. and Mary A. Mitchell still stands today on the corner of Troy Hills Road and Grove Place. Ross Kitchell, who later married Harriet Mitchell, settled in Whippany, carrying on the Kitchell family name in town. (Photograph courtesy of Donald C. Kitchell.)

A heavy snowfall has several parishioners shoveling snow at Our Lady of Mercy Chapel on Whippany Road in February 1962. From the looks of it, these folks have their work cut out for them in the days before most people had their own snow blowers. (Photograph courtesy of Tony Russomanno.)

Ten

Greetings from Hanover Township

The "Old Mill Race" at the entrance to Hanover Mill at Whippany Road and Route 10 has an unspoiled, rustic beauty to it in this turn-of-the-century postcard view. (Photograph courtesy of the collection of Steven Hepler.)

This postcard shows the Agar estate on Route 10 West in Whippany. The exact location is not quite known and should be in the area of the present-day Amoco station. Calvin Agar, who once owned the Box Shop—later International Paper—on Parsippany Road, was also one of the first shareholders of the First National Bank of Whippany. (Photograph courtesy of the collection of R.F. Krygoski.)

The Falls of the Whippany River, located just off Whippany Road from Route 10, are seen in this turn-of-the-century postcard. The falls also fed the raceway for the Hanover Mill. (Photograph courtesy of the collection of Steven Hepler.)

The American House, seen here c. 1890s, was originally located on Route 10 West just east of Troy Hills Road. This large home, which also served as a hotel, was situated along a dirt road that ran through the township. We assume the old hotel could be compared to the popular bed and breakfasts of today. (Photograph courtesy of the collection of R.F. Krygoski.)

The Presbyterian Manse was once located on Route 10 on the corner of Troy Hills Road (at the present site of Molly Malone's, originally a diner). When the diner was built in the mid-50s, the house was relocated around the corner on Troy Hills Road and eventually razed. (Photograph courtesy of the collection of R.F. Krygoski.)

From 1914 through 1940, this building located on Route 10 West next to the Gibraltar Bank building housed the Whippany Post Office. The structure, still standing today, has been noticeably remodeled. A second floor has been added as a private residence. (Photograph courtesy of the collection of R.F. Krygoski.)

We wish we could step right into this postcard and get a closer glimpse of life in Whippany in 1907. We are looking north up Thomas Street and the bridge in front of us traverses the Whippany River. Next is the main line of the Morristown & Erie, which curiously is vacant of any warning signs. The far bridge spans Stony Brook. In the distance is Myron Lee's Grocery and to the right is the post office and Whippanong Hall. (Photograph courtesy of Hanover Township Landmark Committee.)

Thomas Street, Whippany, N. J.

Willie has been very busy and will write you later

1429

This quaint, two-lane dirt road in Whippany was once called Thomas Street. This section of Thomas Street between Whippany Road and Mount Pleasant Avenue is now Parsippany Road. Nobediah Thomas, for whom the street was named, owned a cotton mill in town and lived in the present-day home of the Krygoski family. Looking down the street you can also see the Caladonian Mill before it was destroyed by fire. (Photograph courtesy of the collection of R.F. Krygoski.)

John Martin's Residence Whippany N.J. Formerly Whippany Hotel

The Martin House, once located on the corner of Route 10 West and Troy Hills Road, was also a hotel. History tells us that the Marquis de Lafayette and Major Caleb Gibbs, commander of Washington's personal guard, stopped here for tea before meeting Washington in Morristown. At that time the establishment was called Tappens Tavern. The Martin House later became Parsons Still, an upscale restaurant, and then in the early 1970s it was razed by fire. (Photograph courtesy of the collection of R.F. Krygoski.)

This c. 1960 aerial view of Whippany looks towards the east. The eye travels to Bell Labs, the huge office complex dominating the right center of the photograph. Slightly above it and to the left along the banks of the Whippany River is the Hanover Mill. In the lower center of the scene is the International Paper Company's mill on Parsippany Road. Just across the street, a large forested area can be seen. Today the woods have been leveled and in their place stand the

Oak Ridge Condominiums. Route 10 is the band of concrete that divides the picture. To the left of center, one can find the First Presbyterian Church, the Whippany depot, and Memorial School. To the east, the development of Route 10 through East Hanover has yet to begin. (Photograph courtesy of Morristown & Erie Railway.)

The most difficult photograph to acquire for this book was this picture of Anthony "Tony" Russomanno. Tony, who was always on the other side of the camera, poses here for his son at Yankee Stadium. Tony had a press pass for the ballpark and would be at many games snapping shots of the players. We owe a world of thanks to Tony for all his photographs used in this book. (Photograph courtesy of Anthony Russomanno Jr.)

The authors take time out from collecting pictures and having them identified to pose for a photograph. Bob (left) and Steve are seen here on the front porch of Bob's home on Parsippany Road, an 1830s farmhouse originally built by Nobediah Thomas and later owned by the Fables family. (Photograph courtesy of Susan J. Braviak.)